COMPARING ANIMAL TRAITS

AFRICAN ELEPHANTS

MASSIVE TUSKED MAMMALS

REBECCA E. HIRSCH

Lerner Publications ◆ Minneapolis

Lerner Publications Company
A division of Lerner Publishing Group, Inc.
241 First Avenue North
Minneapolis, MN 55401 USA

For reading levels and more information, look up this title at www.lernerbooks.com.

Photo Acknowledgments

The images in this book are used with the permission of: © Maggy Meyer/Shutterstock.com, p. 1; © GibasDigiPhoto/iStock/Thinkstock, p. 4; © Latitudestock/Getty Images, p. 5; © iStockphoto.com/ AlesVeluscek, p. 6; © Martin Harvey/Photolibrary/Getty Images, p. 7; © Jez Bennett/Shutterstock.com, p. 8 (left); © Bartosz Budrewicz/Shutterstock.com, p. 8 (right); © Volodymyr Burdiak/Shutterstock.com, p. 9 (top); © Martin Withers/FLPA/Getty Images, p. 9 (bottom); © Merlin D. Tutle/Getty Images, p. 10; © David Fettes/Cultura/Getty Images, p. 11 (left); © Margarita Steinhardt, p. 11 (right); © Heinrich van den Berg/ Oxford Scientific/Getty Images, p. 13; © Marc Guitard/Moment Open/Getty Images, pp. 14, 15 (top); © Britta Kasholm-Tengve/E+/Getty Images, p. 15 (bottom right); © Robert Harding Picture Library Ltd/Alamy, p. 15 (left); © Jaime Grill/Getty Images, p. 16; © iStockphoto.com/Lindsay Basson, p. 17 (left); Design Pics/ Ed Robinson/Newscom, p. 17 (right); © Fabian von Poser/Getty Images, p. 18; © Martin Harvey 2004/ Getty Images, p. 19 (top); © Christopher Scott/Gallo Images/Getty Images, p. 19 (bottom); © J & C Sohns/ Picture Press/Getty Images, p. 20; © David Cayless/Getty Images, p. 21 (left); © Westend 61 GmbH/Alamy, p. 21 (right); © Edo Schmidt/Alamy, p. 22; © animalimagery.co.uk/Alamy, p. 23 (top); © Don Johnston/All Canada Photos/Getty Images, p. 23 (bottom); © Sergio Pitamitz//Robert Harding World Imagery/Getty Images, pp. 24, 25; © Anup Shah/Stone/Getty Images, p. 26; © De Agostini/Getty Images, p. 27 (bottom); © iStockphoto.com/EcoPic, p. 27 (top); AP Photo/Ronald Wittek, p. 28; © Rick & Nora Bowers/Alamy, p. 29 (right); © Peter Barritt/Alamy, p. 29 (left).

Front cover: © iStockphoto.com/NightOwlZA.
Back cover © Amy Nichole Harris/Shutterstock.com.

Main body text set in Calvert MT Std 12/18. Typeface provided by Monotype Typography.

Library of Congress Cataloging-in-Publication Data

Hirsch, Rebecca E., author.
    African elephants : massive tusked mammals / by Rebecca E. Hirsch.
      pages   cm. — (Comparing animal traits)
    Includes index.
    ISBN 978-1-4677-5576-4 (lib. bdg. : alk. paper)
    ISBN 978-1-4677-6059-1 (pbk.)
    ISBN 978-1-4677-6215-1 (EB pdf)
    1. African elephant—Juvenile literature. I. Title.
  QL737.P98H55 2015
  599.67′4—dc23
                                                    2014025210

Manufactured in the United States of America
1 — BP —12/31/14

TABLE OF CONTENTS

MEET THE AFRICAN ELEPHANT

A family of African elephants gathers in a shallow river. The young elephants wrestle in the mud and grab sticks with their trunks. As the young elephants play, the adults keep a careful watch. African elephants are a kind of animal called a mammal. Other kinds of animals include insects, fish, amphibians, reptiles, and birds.

African elephants play in the mud.

African elephants are vertebrates and have warm blood, just like all mammals.

Mammals belong to a larger group of animals called vertebrates. All vertebrates have backbones. Mammals are warm-blooded, which means they can keep their bodies warm even in cold weather. All mammals have hair or fur on their bodies. All mammal mothers make milk for their babies. African elephants are similar to other mammals in many ways. But African elephants also have traits that make them unique.

CHAPTER 1
WHAT DO AFRICAN ELEPHANTS LOOK LIKE?

The African elephant is a huge mammal with gray skin, enormous tusks, and a long trunk. Adult males (or bulls) can weigh as much as 14,000 pounds (6,350 kilograms). Females (or cows) reach about half that weight. African elephants are the largest living animals on land.

Both male and female elephants have tusks. Tusks are a kind of teeth. They grow longer as the elephant grows older. African elephants use their tusks to dig for water in dry riverbeds. They also use tusks to defend themselves.

DID YOU KNOW?
ASIAN ELEPHANTS

have smaller bodies than African elephants. An Asian elephant's back is rounded, but an African elephant's back dips in between the animal's shoulders and hips.

African elephants use their long trunks to smell, breathe, find food, suck up water, and greet other elephants. Two **projections** at the tip of the trunk act like fingers. An elephant can lift whole trees or pick up very small objects. The ears let heat escape the elephant's body. This helps the animal keep cool under the blazing African sun.

Male African elephants measure from 20 to 24 feet (6 to 7.3 meters) in length. Female African elephants usually measure about 2 feet (0.6 m) less than that.

AFRICAN ELEPHANT VS. WHITE RHINOCEROS

A white rhinoceros munches grass with its head low to the ground. Its pointy horns stick forward. White rhinoceroses live in southern Africa. They are one of the biggest animals on land. The only larger land animal is an elephant. An adult male rhino can weigh up to 5,070 pounds (2,300 kg). As with African elephants, female white rhinos are smaller than males.

African elephants and white rhinoceroses look similar. Like an African elephant, the white rhinoceros has gray, wrinkly skin and an enormous head. Both animals are nearly hairless. The white rhino has a few hairs on its body and a tuft of hair at the tip of its tail.

An African elephant (*left*) and a white rhino (*right*) both have gray, wrinkly skin.

The white rhino doesn't have tusks, but it does have two horns on its head. The front horn is bigger than the back horn. White rhinos use their horns to defend themselves or their young. They use their flexible upper lips to pick fruit and leaves.

Two white rhinos fight.

9

AFRICAN ELEPHANTS VS. BUMBLEBEE BATS

Bumblebee bats roost upside down in caves and come out at night to hunt. These tiny bats live in Thailand. They are among the smallest mammals in the world. Each bat is about the size of a large bumblebee and weighs less than a penny.

Bumblebee bats are not only smaller than African elephants. They also look very different. African elephants have almost no hair. Bumblebee bats are covered with fur. Brown or gray fur coats their backs, and paler fur coats their bellies.

Elephants have long trunks, but bumblebee bats have fleshy snouts. While elephants travel on their stout legs, bumblebee bats can fly. The bumblebee bat can even hover in the air like a hummingbird by beating its wings fast.

Most bumblebee bats are smaller than a human thumb.

COMPARE IT!

AFRICAN ELEPHANTS

BUMBLEBEE BATS

AFRICAN ELEPHANTS		BUMBLEBEE BATS
18 TO 24.5 FEET (5.4 TO 7.5 M)	◄ HEAD AND BODY LENGTH ►	**1 TO 1.3 INCHES** (29 TO 33 MILLIMETERS)
5,000 TO 14,000 POUNDS (2,268 TO 6,350 KG)	◄ MAXIMUM WEIGHT ►	**0.05 TO 0.07 OUNCES** (1.5 TO 2 GRAMS)

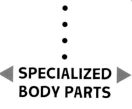

Trunk, for drinking and grasping	◄ SPECIALIZED BODY PARTS ►	Wings, for flight

CHAPTER 2

WHERE DO AFRICAN ELEPHANTS LIVE?

African elephants roam through a wide range of habitats in Africa. You can find them in savannas, forests, and mountains. They also inhabit beaches and deserts. The weather in all of these places is hot.

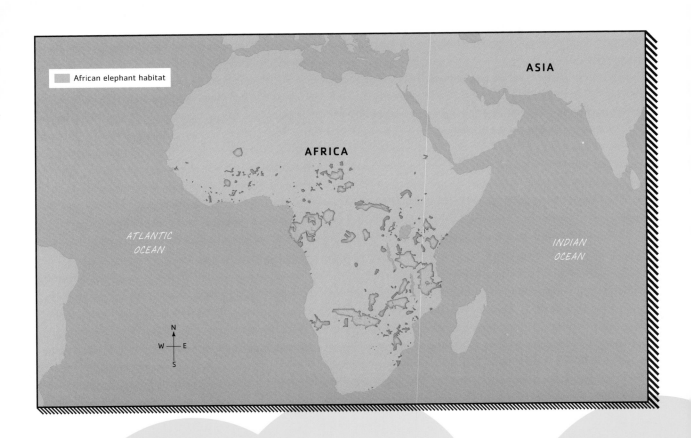

ASIA

African elephant habitat

AFRICA

ATLANTIC OCEAN

INDIAN OCEAN

N
W E
S

African elephants are herbivores, or plant eaters. They spend their days moving through different habitats in search of food and water. These massive mammals have enormous appetites. During the rainy season, food and water are plentiful on the savanna. But during the dry season, African elephants travel in herds to find enough to eat and drink. They leave the savanna and migrate to forested lakes and riverbanks. African elephants are good at remembering where food and water can be found at different times of the year.

Huge numbers of elephants once dwelled in Africa. But their population has fallen in the last several decades. Some people kill elephants for their ivory tusks. People have also turned elephant habitats into farmland. Loss of habitat is a great threat to African elephants.

AFRICAN ELEPHANTS VS. WILDEBEESTS

Wildebeests live in some of the same habitats as African elephants. Noisy herds of these mammals cross savannas and open woodlands in southern Africa. Short grasses grow in the savannas where wildebeests live. Wildebeests graze on these grasses both day and night. If grass is hard to find, wildebeests may snack on the leaves of the scattered trees that grow in the savanna.

Wildebeests graze in an African savanna.

Like African elephants, wildebeests migrate each year. In the rainy season, wildebeests eat their fill in lush pastures. They sip water from rivers and streams. But in May or June, southern Africa's dry season begins. The grass withers, and the rivers dry up. Wildebeests travel in large herds, heading north to greener pastures in central Africa. In fall and winter, they head south again, arriving in time for the rains.

African elephants (*left*) and wildebeests (*right*) both migrate in herds.

AFRICAN ELEPHANTS VS. HAWAIIAN MONK SEALS

Hawaiian monk seals live near islands in the Pacific Ocean. They have a very different habitat than African elephants. African elephants move across many different types of land. Hawaiian monk seals swim in warm tropical waters.

While you can find African elephants across the continent of Africa, Hawaiian monk seals live only in the Hawaiian Islands. And while African elephants migrate, Hawaiian monk seals don't travel far. Most monk seals stay close to the island where they were born. At night, they dive into coral reefs to hunt. The seals eat fish, lobsters, octopuses, and eels. During the day, the seals come to land and sleep on beaches.

Hawaiian monk seals face different threats than African elephants. The seals must avoid sharks. They can also get tangled in fishing lines. Another problem is lack of food. People or other predators may take so many fish from the ocean that the seals can't find enough to eat. In recent years, Hawaiian monk seals have been at risk of extinction.

A Hawaiian monk seal sunbathes on the beach.

COMPARE IT!

AFRICAN ELEPHANTS

HAWAIIAN MONK SEALS

SAVANNAS, MOUNTAINS, FORESTS, DESERTS ◀ HABITAT ▶ **TROPICAL OCEANS**

AFRICA ◀ GEOGRAPHIC RANGE ▶ **HAWAIIAN ISLANDS**

Plants ◀ MAIN FOOD ▶ Fish, lobsters, octopuses, eels

CHAPTER 3

LIFE IN THE ELEPHANT HERD

Female African elephants and their young offspring live in families called herds. The oldest female leads the family. She guides the herd to food and water and steers them away from danger. When the herd is threatened, the adults will circle around the youngsters to protect them from harm.

Bull elephants live in separate herds with other males. Bulls also sometimes live alone. African elephant families often join up with other families. These large herds migrate long distances together. Male and female herds travel separately.

An elephant herd follows its leader toward food and water.

Elephants in a family wrap their trunks together to say hello. They flap their ears to warn of danger. They trumpet loud calls with their trunks. African elephants also communicate with high squeaks and deep rumbles. The rumbles travel through the ground. Other elephants can sense the sounds with their feet or by laying their trunks on the ground.

Two African elephants use their trunks to greet each other.

Elephants communicate by calling out with their trunks.

AFRICAN ELEPHANTS VS. BOTTLENOSE DOLPHINS

Bottlenose dolphins jump and play in warm water.

A bottlenose dolphin leaps out of the water. It lands with a splash. Bottlenose dolphins swim in warm waters around the world. Even though bottlenose dolphins live in different habitats than African elephants, the two mammals share some surprising behaviors.

Both African elephants and bottlenose dolphins live in groups. A group of bottlenose dolphins, called a pod, has about a dozen animals. Similar to elephant herds, multiple pods sometimes travel together. Several pods of dolphins are called a super-pod.

Like African elephants, bottlenose dolphins send messages to one another using body language and sound. Bottlenose dolphins snap their jaws or slap the water with their tails. They call to one another with squeaks and whistles. Each dolphin can be recognized by its whistle. Dolphins may whistle to say hello, warn others of danger, or let other dolphins know food is nearby.

COMPARE IT!

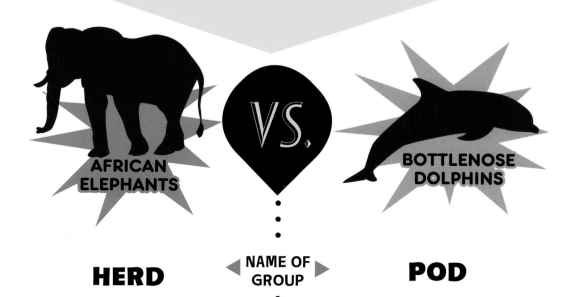

AFRICAN ELEPHANTS

VS.

BOTTLENOSE DOLPHINS

HERD	◀ NAME OF GROUP ▶	POD
9 TO 11	◀ NUMBER OF ANIMALS IN GROUP ▶	**2 TO 15**

Rumbles, squeaks, trumpeting	◀ SOUNDS USED TO COMMUNICATE ▶	Whistles, squeaks

AFRICAN ELEPHANTS VS. SNOW LEOPARDS

A snow leopard climbs silently over rocks in search of prey. The leopard rubs its cheek against a ledge before moving on. Snow leopards live in the snowy mountains of central Asia. These shy cats behave quite differently than African elephants.

African elephants are social, plant-eating animals. But snow leopards are solitary hunters. A mother snow leopard will travel with her cubs. A male and a female will pair up during mating season. But snow leopards come together at few other times. They often live alone.

Snow leopards take care of their young. But otherwise, a snow leopard usually travels by itself.

Because African elephants live together, they communicate with body language and sound. But snow leopards live far apart. To send a message, a snow leopard scratches the ground or sprays urine on rocks. It rubs its cheek against a rock, leaving its scent behind. These markings warn other snow leopards to stay away. They also help male and female cats find each other during mating season.

A snow leopard is a fierce protector of its territory.

CHAPTER 4

THE LIFE CYCLE OF AFRICAN ELEPHANTS

An African elephant begins life as a 265-pound (120 kg) infant. The baby elephant is brown and hairy at birth. Like all mammals, the elephant drinks milk from its mother. Milk helps the baby elephant grow quickly. The calf drinks with its mouth, not its trunk. The calf and its mother stay close to each other during this stage of life.

A young elephant calf drinks its mother's milk.

An adult African elephant never stops GROWING. This mammal keeps getting bigger throughout its life.

At six months, the calf is ready for solid food. It reaches its trunk inside its mother's mouth to take food she has found. Later, adult elephants in the herd show the growing calf what to eat and where to find food and water.

An African elephant **matures** in ten to twelve years. Females stay with the group. Males move away to live with other males. The adult elephants carry traits from their parents, such as massive bodies and tusks. With these traits, the African elephant can survive for as long as seventy years.

AFRICAN ELEPHANTS VS. ORANGUTANS

Orangutans swing from tree to tree in the rain forests of Asia. Orangutans live in a different habitat than African elephants, but the two mammals have similar life cycles. African elephants and orangutans both give birth to one baby at a time. Both animal babies stay close to their mothers. An African elephant mother and her calf stay about a trunk's reach apart. A young orangutan clings to its mother's body as the mother travels through the forest.

An infant orangutan clings to its mother's back during travel.

Young orangutans drink their mother's milk, as all mammals do. Orangutans nurse for three to four years, the same length of time as African elephants. Young orangutans spend eight years learning from their mothers before they are ready to strike out on their own, compared with ten to twelve years for African elephants. They must learn a lot to stay alive in the forest. Orangutans in the wild can survive more than fifty years, nearly as long as African elephants.

Young African elephants (*top*) and orangutans (*bottom*) both stay with their parents for years before becoming independent.

AFRICAN ELEPHANTS VS. VIRGINIA OPOSSUMS

Virginia opossums scramble through forests in North America. These cat-sized mammals hang upside down from trees when they are young. Virginia opossums behave differently than African elephants. They also have different life cycles.

African elephants give birth to one calf at a time. But female opossums can give birth to more than a dozen babies. A newborn African elephant weighs more than most humans and walks soon after birth. But newborn opossums are the size of bumblebees. They are blind and ride in their mother's special pouch.

African elephants grow up more slowly than Virginia opossums. Elephant calves drink milk for three or four years. They aren't ready to live on their own for at least ten years. But Virginia opossums stop drinking milk and are ready to live on their own after only three months. Unlike the long life span of African elephants, the life span of a Virginia opossum is about two years.

COMPARE IT!

AFRICAN ELEPHANTS

VS.

VIRGINIA OPPOSSUMS

AFRICAN ELEPHANTS		VIRGINIA OPPOSSUMS
1	◀ AVERAGE NUMBER OF ▶ YOUNG AT BIRTH	**8**
265 POUNDS (120 KG)	◀ SIZE OF NEWBORN ▶ AT BIRTH	**0.005 OUNCES** (0.13 G)
77 YEARS	◀ TYPICAL ▶ LIFE SPAN	**2 YEARS**

AFRICAN ELEPHANT TRAIT CHART

This book explored the ways African elephants are similar to and different from other mammals. What other mammals would you like to learn about?

	WARM-BLOODED	HAIR ON BODY	GIVE BIRTH TO LIVE YOUNG	TUSKS OR HORNS	WIDESPREAD HABITAT	LIVE IN GROUPS
AFRICAN ELEPHANT	X	X	X	X	X	X
WHITE RHINOCEROS	X	X	X	X	X	X
BUMBLEBEE BAT	X	X	X		X	
WILDEBEEST	X	X	X	X	X	X
HAWAIIAN MONK SEAL	X	X	X			
BOTTLENOSE DOLPHIN	X	X	X		X	X
SNOW LEOPARD	X	X	X			
ORANGUTAN	X	X	X			
VIRGINIA OPOSSUM	X	X	X		X	

GLOSSARY

Afrikaans: a language spoken mainly in the nations of South Africa and Namibia

coral reefs: ridges near the surface of water, made up of a stony substance that certain forms of marine life create

extinction: the state of no longer existing

habitats: environments where an animal naturally lives. A habitat is the place where an animal can find food, water, air, shelter, and a place to raise its young.

herbivores: plant-eating animals

matures: reaches adulthood

migrate: to move from one place to another

population: all the animals of one type

predators: animals that hunt, or prey on, other animals

projections: things that stick out from a surface

savannas: grasslands containing scattered trees

social: living in groups or communities

solitary: living by itself

traits: features that are inherited from parents. Body size and fur color are examples of inherited traits.

LERNER

SOURCE

Expand learning beyond the printed book. Download free, complementary educational resources for this book from our website, www.lerneresource.com.

SELECTED BIBLIOGRAPHY

"African Elephant (*Loxodonta africana*)." Wildscreen. June 10, 2014. http://www.arkive.org/african-elephant/loxodonta-africana/.

"African Elephant Fact Sheet." World Wildlife Fund. June 10, 2014. http://assets.panda.org/downloads/african_elephant_factsheet2007w.pdf.

Blanc, J. "*Loxodonta africana*." IUCN 2013. IUCN Red List of Threatened Species. June 10, 2014. http://www.iucnredlist.org.

"Fascinating Facts about Elephants at Tembe Elephant National Park." Tembe Elephant Park. June 16, 2014. http://www.africaelephants.com/elephant_facts.htm.

"Scientists Unravel the Secret World of Elephant Communication." Phys.org. June 18, 2014. http://phys.org/news4211.html.

FURTHER INFORMATION

Carney, Elizabeth. *Great Migrations: Whales, Wildebeests, Butterflies, Elephants, and Other Amazing Animals on the Move.* Washington, DC: National Geographic, 2010. Read this book to get a close-up look at the migration of African elephants and many other kinds of animals that migrate.

The Elephant Listening Project—Forest Elephant Talk
http://www.birds.cornell.edu/brp/elephant/cyclotis/language/eletalk.html
Visitors to this site from the Cornell Lab of Ornithology can listen to some of the many different calls of African elephants.

O'Connell, Caitlin, and Donna M. Jackson. *The Elephant Scientist.* Boston: Houghton Mifflin Books for Children, 2011. Pick up this book to learn how scientists made a breakthrough discovery about the ways elephants communicate.

Wildscreen Arkive: African Elephant
http://www.arkive.org/african-elephant/loxodonta-africana/video-17c.html
Watch this footage from the wildlife group Wildscreen to see a family of African elephants help a newborn elephant to its feet for the first time.

Wojahn, Rebecca Hogue, and Donald Wojahn. *A Savanna Food Chain: A Who-Eats-What Adventure in Africa.* Minneapolis: Lerner Publications, 2009. Learn more about the food chains in an African savanna with the help of this book.

INDEX